Adva
The Adventu

"*Jim Melvin's spirited the '60s in Florida epitomize the essence of the enduring magic of a special place.* Florida Boy *shares the secret to its discovery in this book. Find it outside; in a splendid world available, year-round, to anyone seeking its natural treasures. Florida's ever-changing diverse and rich wetlands, dynamic coastlines, magnificent seas, abundant marine life, splendid forests, and exciting wildlife are right there, just past the front door, in the great 'outside.'"* —Mark Loyacano

"*Mark me down as someone who thinks you spin a good yarn.*" —Caro Henry

"*Wonderfully descriptive memories. Each one captures the time and place perfectly.*" —Daniel O'Donnell

"*Your writing takes me back to my own childhood. A magical time, indeed.*" —Wendy Parciak

"*Really enjoyed this. Roy Orbison, and toy soldiers with parachutes, yeah! We've had similar experiences. Thanks for the memories!!*" —James Ron

"Having moved from Jamaica to South Florida at 15, I've now lived here for nearly fifty years. Florida stories are rare treasures, and Jim Melvin's boyhood memories capture something genuine about this place I now call home." —**Dale Mahfood**

"Ah, this brings back memories. ... Sometimes I wonder if kids these days have these kinds of experiences anymore or if they're all glued to their screens."
—**Alexander Ipfelkofer**

"I loved every story. I felt like I was there, sweating in the heat, humidity AND the height of those branches. I was a daredevil back then as well, but now I can't even stand on a chair without vertigo. Terrific writing."
—**Geno Scala**

"These wonderful pieces come together to paint a picturesque, touching story. Keep painting, the grittier and tougher and more unvarnished the better!"
—**Joshua Shapiro**

"Such wholesome times! I'm sad for children growing up today." —**Nadia Gerassimenko**

"Dropping twenty feet from a tree astounds me. We flew from a Tarzan swing rope that high but leaped into

space to flip and dive into a lake over and over. I've been enjoying your time-leaps and your pine pitch that sticks to my fingers." —**Richard Blaisdell**

"This is a feel-good memoir about a free-range childhood in the 1960s." —**Isabelle Fetherston**

"Jim's childhood memories were my childhood memories. I've always said we had three seasons growing up: baseball season, football season, and saltwater season. We were always swimming, fishing, skiing, bridge-jumping or hanging with friends at the beach. The unsupervised freedom was taken for granted and it was how we enjoyed ourselves. I have enjoyed reading every chapter of Jim's book and reliving my childhood. I believe the kids of our generation would change very little, if anything. It is fun being carried back to that time. Thanks for that, Jim." —**Guy Shanahan**

"A joyous glimpse into a childhood we all wish we'd had: fun, carefree, and near the sea." —**JS Hyder**

The
Adventures
of a
Florida Boy

*In the 1960s, kids ran as far and wild
as their imaginations would take them*

Jim Melvin

Copyright © 2025 by Jim Melvin

All rights reserved. No part of this book may be used or reproduced in any form whatsoever without written permission except in the case of brief quotations in critical articles or reviews.

This is a work of nonfiction. All the events described here are true to the best of the author's memory. Some names and identifying features may have been changed or omitted to protect the identity of certain parties. The views expressed in this work are solely those of the author.

Printed in the United States of America.
Cover art/design: miblart.com
Interior stock art: depositphotos.com
Author photo: Jeanne Malmgren

ISBN: 979-8-9924922-0-0
Green Bird Publishing
First Edition: January 2025

Contact:
jimmelvin57@gmail.com

Or visit:
jimmelvin.substack.com
jim-melvin.com

Author's note

Times have changed, though I'm not one of those who says all change is for the worse. There has been some good, some bad, and a lot of the same old same old.

But as I write this now, in late 2024, there is a bit too much chaos for my tastes. Our politics are divisive, wars are raging, severe weather events are wreaking havoc, and on top of all that, each of us has our own set of personal difficulties that comes with being an adult.

Many of us are in dire need of relief. We're like people on a strict diet who occasionally cast aside our discipline and devour a pint of ice cream for the pure pleasure of it. We can't exist on sorrow alone. Sometimes we search for something good-natured and humorous to lift our spirits and put a smile on our faces.

This is what *The Adventures of a Florida Boy* is all about. It's a short and sweet memoir that won't challenge your beliefs or try to change your opinions.

Rather, I'm hoping it makes you laugh and puts a warm feeling in your stomach. I also hope it revives memories of your own childhood wherever and whenever you grew up. If you're in the mood for a lighthearted read that will lift your spirits, *The Adventures of a Florida Boy* fits the bill.

Some of you might know me already. I'm an award-winning novelist who has specialized in epic fantasy. My latest series is *Dark Circles*, a teen adventure for ages 13 and older. But I'm also known for *The Death Wizard Chronicles*, a six-book epic fantasy for mature audiences.

Writing about fantastical worlds isn't easy for everyone, but for me it's a piece of cake. My larger-than-life imagination was seared into my brain during my childhood growing up in the 1960s in Florida, and as the subtitle of my memoir suggests, the Sixties was a far different time than today. Kids really did run as far and wild as their imaginations took them. All we needed was a Pop-Tart for breakfast and a peanut butter and jelly sandwich (on Wonder Bread) for lunch, and we were good to go.

We'd throw on T-shirts and shorts and rush out our front doors into a world of wonders. Some of the things we did—climbing towering trees, swimming in surging seas, riding our bikes to faraway places—were downright dangerous. We didn't care. We were the rulers of our domain.

I wouldn't trade my childhood for anything. I wouldn't trade my imagination, either.

I hope you feel the same.

CONTENTS

Prologue	1
Interlude I	5
The Shark	6
By Land and by Sea	12
Creatures Large and Small	18
Interlude II	24
The Ravioli Incident	26
'I'm Doomed!'	31
The Diving Bell	35
Interlude III	41
The Spider Monkey	43
The Dogs of Coquina Key	47
Gators, Roaches and More	55
Interlude IV	66
Safety Patrol	67
The Toad	71
All My Jobs	76
Interlude V	86
The Ultimate Drop	88
Catch of a Lifetime	92
Up, Up and Away	98
Interlude VI	104
The Giant SweeTART	105
Facing My Demons	109
Life-Saver	114
Epilogue	119

PROLOGUE

Most of my boyhood in the 1960s was spent in Florida on an island called Coquina Key. My parents' waterfront home in St. Petersburg overlooked a broad expanse of Tampa Bay. Back then, sizable portions of the island were undeveloped, which provided plenty of places to climb trees, dig forts in the sand, and swim in shark-infested waters, though we were too young and fearless to give the latter much consideration.

I was lucky to have friends near my age who lived on my street only a few houses away. On a typical Saturday afternoon, there could be anywhere from two to ten of us, depending on who was around.

A non-school day typically looked like this:

- Leap out of bed.
- Scarf a sugary breakfast.
- Rush outside.
- Play with friends until noon.
- Zip inside for a sandwich, Lay's potato chips, and a cold glass of moo juice.
- Run back out the door.
- Play with friends until dinnertime.
- Rush in the house to eat a quick dinner (ravioli was my favorite, as you'll soon learn).
- Scramble back out the door.
- Play with friends until dark.
- Return home and go to bed without even taking a shower.

I know this is a cliché, but back then there were no video games, smartphones, or laptops. Whatever intelligence I had was real, not artificial. When I went out to play, I went *out* to play.

Every day, my friends and I would invent something new to entertain ourselves.

Maybe we were knights in shining armor

wielding sticks as swords and garbage-can lids as shields.

Maybe we dug elaborate underground forts and covered them with plywood and a layer of sand to conceal them from the rest of the world.

Maybe we were deep-sea divers, swimming WAYYY too far out into Tampa Bay and then seeing how deep we could go on one breath. When one of us reached the lightless bottom and came up with a handful of seaweed and muck, we called it "proof," as in proof you had made it all the way down. Kids our age didn't take another kid's word for much of anything. "Proof" was a requirement. Our daily physical activities were too fiercely competitive to rely solely on trust.

Maybe we jumped on our bikes and rode for miles all over town, often on congested roads with heavy traffic. I did this—mostly with friends but sometimes alone—when I was as young as 8.

Lost in Space was a popular TV show. We acted that one out a lot. A tubby friend of mine was the robot. Even though I was the skinniest kid, I often was the leader, assuming the role of Dr. John Robinson.

The earliest James Bond movies were also popular, but everybody wanted to be James, so our spy games were more generic.

The scary vampire TV show *Dark Shadows* was another favorite. My friends and I slew a lot of vampires—in broad daylight.

Other popular shows included *Mission Impossible*, *The Outer Limits*, and *The Man From U.N.C.L.E.* I was always the dark and handsome Napoleon Solo, even though I had white-blond hair. I once talked my mom into dyeing my hair brown so I could look like Napoleon, but after a couple of shampoos the cheap hair dye turned green. I was ahead of my time.

And of course, we played every sport imaginable: baseball, basketball, football, kickball, even kill-the-carrier.

My imagination was born during a time when children ran wild—and when "wild" didn't mean crime, drugs, or sex. It meant *in the wild*.

INTERLUDE I

I'm walking to school on a cool winter morning. Though I'm only 7 years old and in second grade, I'm alone on a cement pathway that winds through several acres of forest. This is the quickest way to get to school on foot. Circumventing the thick woods would add twenty minutes to my walk. Billows of white mist burst from my mouth, which is uncommon in Florida where winter is a fleeting thing. I come to a sudden halt. Lying in the center of the path, a stone's throw in front of me, looms a massive rattlesnake. It stares at me but doesn't move, probably more stunned by the cold than I. My little body freezes in place, both figuratively and literally, and I'm not sure what to do. I look around for help, but there's no one in sight. I finally decide to wend off the path through a razor-sharp tangle of saw palmettos and work my way around the beast, which barely moves except for swiveling its head and watching me. I re-enter the path a safe distance away and continue toward school. I never tell anyone about the snake. Until now.

THE SHARK

One of the advantages of growing up on Tampa Bay was that I was always only a few steps away from a place to go saltwater fishing. When I turned 12, I made a lot of money for a kid my age mowing lawns all around Coquina Key (stay tuned) and spent much of my cash on fishing equipment. I had three rigs—huge, medium, and small—and a tackle box stuffed with every imaginable weight, hook, bobber, and lure.

I caught many different varieties of fish, but I prized snook the most. They were called linesiders because of the black line that ran from their head to tail. Snook that weighed between 5 and 15 pounds ranked among the most delicious saltwater fish in the sea. But the only snook I ever ate were caught by someone else. I could never seem to hook a single one.

During the school year, I often did my homework in our backyard screened porch that overlooked Tampa Bay. While studying math, science, and English, I also fished—the Sixties version of multitasking. After arranging my books, papers, and pencils on the wrought-iron table, I went to our garage and brought out my smallest and largest rigs. I first attached a tiny piece of hotdog to the hook of my small rig and cast a line off the seawall. In only a few seconds I reeled in a hand-sized pinfish, a favorite bait of anglers in southern waters. Next, I hooked the pinfish to my larger rig, climbed down an extension ladder into knee-deep water at the base of our eight-foot seawall, waded out to where it was waist-deep, and cast the pinfish as far as I could into the deeper channel. Then I trudged back, climbed up the ladder, and slid the butt-end of the fishing pole into the chain-link fence that ran along both sides of our backyard. Satisfied that all was now in order, I went inside the porch and started my homework, glancing at the pole every couple of minutes to see if there was any action.

Half an hour later, I saw the thick pole bend crazily. Holy cow! I had something BIG! Surely it was the snook of all snooks.

I hustled out of the porch, grabbed the pole, and gave it a big yank. Immediately after, a huge fish broke the surface way out in the channel in an explosion of froth.

SNOOK! SNOOK!!! I screamed. But there was no one to hear. My stepdad was still at work and my mom was inside watching the boob tube and smoking cigarettes. There were no neighbors around either. Other than my frenetic shouting, it was as silent as a scene in a post-apocalyptic movie.

The powerful fish almost stripped out all my line, but I had expensive thirty-pound test on this rig that could handle a lot of tension. I tightened the drag and began to pump and reel. It felt like I was hauling in a boulder.

Several times, I retrieved 100 feet of line only to have the fish rip it back out. I wondered if this beast was too large and powerful for even my best rig.

Anyone who has fished a lot knows there are few things worse than having your line snap before you at least get a look at what was on the other end.

I finally wrestled the fish close enough to get a better view. It was indeed huge, which should have excited me, but I realized it was larger even than a world-record snook. It was a shark—at least five feet long and probably eighty pounds. Since there was a sandbar on the other side of the channel, it was most likely a sand shark.

SHARK! SHARK!!! I yelled, hoping this might attract some attention and lure someone outside to witness my epic battle, but the apocalypse had apparently wiped everyone but the shark and me from existence.

After a long fight, I tired the shark enough to bring him to the base of the seawall. But now what? I wasn't about to go down and get in the water with him, but I also didn't have a net big enough to scoop him up. My only option was to muscle him over the top of the seawall.

I leaned forward until the tip of the rod was only

a couple of feet from the shark's head and then pulled back with all my strength. The shark rose out of the water until his head peeked just above the seawall, but he thrashed like a maniac and zipped off enough line to drop into the water. After that, I had another long fight just to get him back to the seawall.

My second effort was more successful. I got half his body over the edge, but he continued to flail about, resembling the great white shark about to devour Quint in the movie *Jaws* (which would hit the big screen seven years later).

The shark fell into the water again, but now he was too tired to fight. I gave it one last heave and got almost three-fourths of his body over the top of the seawall. Just when it appeared I had him, the line snapped. Even then, the shark hung there a moment between land and sea before slipping in slow motion back into the water. I watched him swim wearily away until he disappeared into the darkness of the channel.

In retrospect, I'm glad the shark escaped. If I had caught him, I would've probably put him in a wheelbarrow and showed him off around the neighborhood before tossing his dead body into the bay to be devoured by all manner of creatures. This would have been an ignominious end for such a grand fish.

More than half a century after my epic battle, I still wish the shark well. I hope he survived the rigors of our encounter and enjoyed a long life. They say sand sharks can live as long as forty years.

Whatever the end result, he gave me one heck of a fight that I'll never forget.

BY LAND AND BY SEA

As of this writing, I live in Upstate South Carolina, an area of the U.S. dominated by red clay and lots of roots and rocks. It can take twenty torturous minutes to chop a hole in the ground large enough to plant a small bush. But where I grew up in St. Petersburg, red clay was nonexistent. Sand was the dominant soil type—and not only on the beaches. It was everywhere.

A couple of strong boys with a pair of long shovels could dig a hole five feet wide and deep in about the same time it now takes me to plant the small bush. Unlike a Florida beach, there was only a few inches of wispy sand on the surface of the barren sand fields across the street from my house on Coquina Key. Beneath that it became denser and moist, still easy to dig into but solid enough to not cave in.

Once the hole was dug to our satisfaction, we covered it with a sheet of plywood, sprinkled sand over the wood to hide its location, and voila!—we had a secret fort in which to hatch our devious plans. Well, our plans weren't truly devious, but we pretended like they were.

Though it was usually blazing hot outside, the inside of our underground forts felt blissfully cool. We sat in semi-darkness for long stretches, sometimes even bringing our lunches. The potential of a wall collapsing or anything else dangerous happening didn't register in our young minds. Heck, we were used to burying ourselves in sand up to our necks at the beach, so the forts posed no risk to us.

Sand forts played a substantial role in my boyhood. From age 8 to 15, I helped dig dozens of them. My stepdad's disappearing plywood stockpile must have perplexed him. (Back then, plywood was inexpensive and readily available, so everyone kept a few sheets in their garage. Like most everything else, it's not quite as cheap nowadays.)

Research indicates that playing in dirt has many health benefits. If so, I must have been extremely healthy. I was always dirty, but it was a dry, grainy kind of dirty, not like a blackened coal miner. Until seventh grade, I only took a shower or bath a couple of times a week, so my bed was usually filled with sand, angering my mother and grossing out my sister, neither of whom could understand how I slept that way. I didn't care. Sand was my friend.

(Early in seventh grade, one of the cute girls at school told me that I smelled funny. After that, I showered daily. My family's opinion mattered little, but a cute girl's view of me mattered a lot.)

Ticks were also commonplace. It became an almost daily ritual to pluck them off with a pair of tweezers. None of us knew about Lyme disease, so it was more just an inconvenience than anything else. However, the ticks seemed to treasure a boy's private parts. I don't know why. Maybe the blood tasted better down there. That part of it rose well above the level of inconvenience.

Though it must sound like I was a filthy animal,

I cleaned up occasionally. After spending an hour sequestered in one of our forts, we would go for a swim in Tampa Bay. One of my friends had a long wooden dock in his backyard that extended all the way to the channel. We stripped to our shorts and ran the length of the dock screaming like madmen. Then we leaped off the end of the dock into the channel, flailing our arms and kicking our legs for what seemed like forever before plummeting into the silky-warm saltwater.

The current was so strong, there was no sense in fighting it. Instead, we simply let it take us on a raucous ride before finally dumping us into a nearby canal. It was like tubing down a surging whitewater river and ending up in a calm eddy. Then we waded back to the dock and did it again. Who knows how many times bull sharks checked us out? Or we almost stepped on stingrays? Who cares?

We did most of our swimming in a channel that began a stone's throw from the seawall and extended about 500 feet until it bumped against a wide sandbar. The deepest part of the channel was about fifteen feet, which was fine for recreational boats but not deep enough for the massive tankers that entered Tampa Bay from the Gulf of Mexico on their way to the mega-port in Tampa. These thousand-foot-long behemoths cruised the much-deeper shipping channel that ran through the heart of the bay.

We thought nothing of running around barefoot on the sandbar, which was home to sharks, stingrays, horseshoe crabs, sea cucumbers, anemones, oysters, clams, and poisonous jellyfish. The water was shallow—averaging about two feet—and low tide exposed portions of sand that formed short-lived beaches. We spent hours flopping around out there, dodging what we could see and hoping not to step on what we couldn't. The only thing that intimidated us was the shipping channel that began on the other side of the sandbar. The big sharks were out there, and not just in our imaginations. They were out there for real: bull sharks, blacktips, nurse sharks, and hammerheads.

Speaking of hammerheads, we all feared a legendary one named Old Hitler. Grizzled anglers claimed Old Hitler was a twenty-five-foot man-eater, dark as the devil, and covered with scars. None of us ever saw this monster, but that didn't stop us from shivering at the mere mention of him.

Even with the threat of Old Hitler, we sometimes couldn't help ourselves, and several times we dared to sit on inner tubes and float hundreds of feet from the safety of the sandbar into the shipping channel. We never came close to the tankers, but there were plenty of fins to be seen, though these usually turned out to be curious dolphins. Lucky for us.

If you put me on an inner tube in the middle of Tampa Bay right now, I might cry like a baby. Back then, it was just another adventure. Reckless? Sure. But thrilling, nonetheless.

CREATURES LARGE AND SMALL

As you must have noted by now, I spent a lot of time in and around the sea when I was a boy. Tampa Bay was literally in my backyard, but I also spent countless hours in the bathtub-warm waters of the Gulf of Mexico and often crossed the state with my family or friends to frolic in the slightly cooler Atlantic Ocean. I swam, fished, and zoomed around on boats, encountering a vast array of sea creatures that varied in size from minnows to manta rays.

I can't emphasize enough that I did things when 8 to 15 years old that I wouldn't dare do as a 67-year-old man. Something as simple as walking around barefoot in the brackish waters of Tampa Bay would scare me now. Back then, we thought nothing of it despite a slew of reasons it wasn't wise to walk in waist-deep water when you couldn't see the bottom.

During my aquatic wanderings, there was rarely a time when I didn't see something interesting. Several times a year, humongous schools of mullet—tens of thousands strong—congregated in the channel. The schools were so dense, the mullets' heads were squeezed together and forced above the surface. Dolphins feasted on them, leaping high in the air and crashing down upon their prey. It was so much fun to watch, blowing away anything featured on *National Geographic.*

The mullet also provided a bounty for a boy with a fishing pole and a snatch hook. A Chinese college professor and his wife lived at the end of our road, and they happily paid me good money for a freshly snagged mullet—25 cents a pop! They were accustomed to me knocking on their front door with a still-wriggling fish in a bucket. I loved them. And they loved me. They're most likely both dead now, but in my mind they're frozen in time as adults in their mid-40s.

Remember the dolphins? Well, they were

everywhere! During high tide they came right up to my seawall, turned on their sides, and smiled at me. When I swam in the bay with my friends, dolphins surfaced as close as ten feet away, and despite their formidable size, it didn't scare us. We tried to touch them, but they were far too fast and clever. Our clumsiness must have amused them, like we were swimming in mud.

Though I've already talked a lot about sharks, we didn't see many big ones, to be honest. There were plenty of sand sharks, but they were relatively harmless, so we ignored them. I know there were big sharks lurking in the brackish water, but I never had a close call, at least of which I was aware.

One morning, my friend and I walked onto his dock to have a look around. The tide was extraordinarily low, exposing damp sand usually covered by several feet of water. The temporary beach extended about twenty feet from the seawall to the water's edge. To our amazement, we saw a giant sea turtle the size of the hood of a compact car lying on the sand. We leaped off the dock to investigate, expecting the turtle to scramble away, but when we got a closer look, we saw that its head was bloodied. A shark might have attacked it, but it more likely had been struck by a boat propeller. Either way, it was dead.

We told my friend's parents. They called a wildlife rehabilitation center and asked if its scientists might want to come and get the turtle. Maybe they could study the carcass and eventually put the shell on display. Sure enough, they *were* interested, but they said they couldn't haul it off until late in the afternoon. My friend and I were afraid the tide would come in and wash the turtle away, so we got a thin rope and tied one end to his dock and the other to one of the turtle's fins. After that, we scampered off to play.

Later that day, we returned to check on things. Unbelievably, the turtle was gone but not before it had stretched the rope all the way to the water's edge. The turtle hadn't been dead after all and had crawled back into the bay. This made us happy, though it bemused the aquatic experts.

Of all the marvelous creatures I encountered, one stood above the rest. My sister, then around 17, had a boyfriend with a 26-foot speedboat, and she talked him into taking her, my friend, and me into the Gulf of Mexico for fishing and fun. At one point, we were cruising along when I noticed what appeared to be a pair of sharks swimming side by side about thirty feet apart. The weird thing was, their fins surfaced and then disappeared in unison, over and over. We became curious, so the intrepid boyfriend motored over to see what was up.

What we came upon remains one of the most amazing things I've ever seen. It wasn't a pair of sharks after all. Rather, it was the wing tips of a manta ray that had to be thirty feet wide and long (including its tail), and five feet thick. It probably weighed three tons and might have been one of the largest manta rays in the history of the world.

We approached within a stone's throw. The manta ray, of course, didn't appreciate this, so it swung down one of its massive wings like a dipping jet fighter and disappeared beneath the surface. The resulting suction nearly capsized us.

We followed the immense creature around for more than an hour. They say that cobia—a highly prized sport fish—lurk underneath huge manta rays, eating the scraps the rays leave behind. If you cast onto the ray's back, the bait will roll off the side and get snapped up by the cobia. To be honest, the manta ray was so big we were too scared to cast onto it, not wanting to make it even angrier than it already was.

Eventually, the behemoth dove beneath the surface one last time and disappeared. We hung out for a while, hoping to see it again, but never did.

Back then there was no such thing as smartphones, and we didn't have an ordinary camera with us, so I have no official record of this incredible occurrence other than in my head. Oh, and in the heads of three fellow witnesses.

They say manta rays can live as long as seventy-five years, which means the wondrous creature we saw over fifty years ago might still be alive today. If so, it would be a privilege to see it one last time.

INTERLUDE II

It's time to wash my stepdad's car using a JetX sprayer that attaches to the end of a garden hose. This is one of my weekly chores to earn my allowance, but it's kind of fun. The spray gun has a long wand that emits a powerful blast of soapy water, which makes cleaning the car a snap. I attach the nozzle to the hose, turn on the faucet, and then drag the sprayer from the house to the middle of our driveway. I've done this same thing many times, so no sweat. Only this time when I pull the trigger on the gun, nothing happens. I lay the JetX on the driveway and go back to the faucet to make sure it's on and am puzzled to find that the handle is open as far as it will go. What the heck? I go back to the sprayer, pick it up, and pull the trigger again. Now there's a tiny spurt and something that resembles a rubbery twig comes out the end of the wand. Now I'm really confused. I unscrew the wand from the spray gun and hold the butt end of the nozzle up to my eye to see what's stuck in there. To my horror, the distorted face of a disemboweled lizard is staring at me from inside the nozzle, its mouth so close to my eye that it almost touches my lashes. The lizard must have been hiding inside our garden hose, and the water pressure from the opened faucet had ripped it to shreds. I scream like a fool and hurl the nozzle halfway across the yard. It takes several minutes to disgorge the lizard's remains from the wand. But it takes even longer for my heart to stop pounding out of my chest. I mean, come on!

THE RAVIOLI INCIDENT

For several years my friend and I were members of his parents' church, which had a hyperactive congregation that was always planning extracurricular stuff, from picnics in the park to weekend camping trips. I found the actual church services to be boring, but there was one thing I liked about them. It was always entertaining when it came time to sing a hymn, though it wasn't the singing part that I enjoyed but rather the larger-than-life performances of the "old ladies," as we boys liked to call them. Hymn time was their weekly opportunity to perform in front of a crowd, and they bellowed with enough gusto to shatter the sanctuary's stained-glass windows. This never failed to crack me up.

I remember one of the old ladies—who was standing in a pew one row ahead of me—doing her best impersonation of a world-class opera star. But when the rest of the congregation sang the second stanza, she accidentally repeated the first one. This created a harmonic dissonance that continued for about thirty seconds before she recognized her error. As you might imagine, my friend and I lost it, succumbing to a fit of giggling loud enough to be noticeable throughout the holy chamber. And the more we giggled, the more infectious it became. Eventually, someone had to come over and order us to leave. Luckily, my friend's parents had skipped this service and weren't there to witness our inappropriate behavior, so we escaped without any serious repercussions.

Another time, the congregation gathered at a hotel in downtown St. Petersburg for a festive party that culminated in a potluck dinner served in one of the conference rooms. Before the meal, my friend and I had a blast running around the hotel doing all kinds of crazy stuff. There was even a basketball court on the rooftop, but our spirited game ended when the ball bounced off the roof and fell into the abyss, lost to us forever.

The next thing we knew it was dark outside and time to eat dinner. My friend and I simultaneously realized we were starving.

When we entered the conference room, it pleased us to see a long L-shaped table covered with an impressive assortment of delicious dishes: baked ham, chicken breasts, hot dogs, macaroni and cheese, mashed potatoes, corn on the cob, green beans, cookies, cakes, pies, and puddings. The bad news was over fifty old ladies and old men had arrived before us. My friend and I found ourselves last in an interminably long line. Well, we were almost last. A boy we didn't know, but who looked to be about five years older than us, was the official last person. Lucky him.

I was a 10-year-old with a twenty-inch waist and a fifty-inch appetite. Even as a boy I loved all kinds of foods, including most vegetables. But my all-time favorite was ravioli, and as fate would have it, the last dish at the far end of the table was a steaming pot of the luscious pasta. I looked at it with lust in my heart, but it was maddeningly far away.

The old ladies and men were having a grand old time chatting and laughing, laughing and chatting … chatting, chatting, chatting … laughing, laughing, laughing … *over and over and over and over*, all the while taking *waaaaay* too much time to fill their plates. The line moved in ultra-slow motion, which was a sore trial for a boy about to die from starvation. As my anxiety increased, I considered grabbing the ravioli and making a run for it. Meanwhile, the pot was being emptied one spoonful after another, and there was nothing I could do about it except kick myself for not getting to the dinner sooner.

Fiiiinally, I reached the end of the table and stood above my beloved ravioli, but after all this time there were now only three squares left. I greedily scooped up all that remained, not leaving even a drop of sauce for the older boy behind me.

Soon after, it became obvious he had also coveted the ravioli. He looked down at me with murder in his eyes, his face red as a beet. Drool oozed from the corners of his mouth and inch-long fangs sprouted from his incisors.

The boy then spewed two infamous words engorged with venom potent enough to dissolve steel. I can still hear those words in my mind.

"You-u-u-u-u-u **PIG**!!!!!!!!"

That scared me, but not bad enough to make me surrender the ravioli. I hustled away, hid in a dark corner, and devoured my three precious squares before I touched anything else on my plate.

I often wonder if the boy ever thought about the ravioli incident again. I certainly did. It weighed on my mind for decades to come.

But I still love ravioli. So sue me.

'I'M DOOMED!'

My stepdad was an odd sort. He didn't worry about the big things I might have done, like skipping school or doing drugs. (Not that I did either until I was much older. At the time of this story, I was around 11.) But he was a stickler for little things. For instance, if I was supposed to be home for dinner at 6 o'clock, that did not mean 6:10. If I was a couple of minutes late, he would raise hell. To this day, I'm rarely late for anything. If I'm behind schedule, I'm consumed with anxiety. And I have passed this trait on to my own kids.

Another thing my stepdad didn't like was being forced to tell me something twice. One day my friends and I were throwing a Frisbee in my front yard, and it ended up on the roof of the house. My stepdad let me climb a ladder and get it, but he made it clear to not play with the Frisbee anywhere near the house again.

Of course, I did.

It was approaching dusk in late fall, which in 1960s Florida meant cloudy skies and temperatures in the low 70s. A dozen of my friends and I were messing around in the street in front of my house, tossing a football, dribbling a basketball, and throwing a Frisbee. My stepdad and mom had gone somewhere, but I expected them back soon.

One of my friends caught the Frisbee and then unleashed an epic throw. It spun spectacularly, rose high into the air, and landed dead-center on the front side of our roof. There were audible gasps. All the kids knew how ticked off my stepdad could get, and none of them dared mess with him. He wasn't a physical guy, but his voice was scary.

I did what most kids do in situations like this.

FREAKED OUT!!!

"Why'd you throw it up there???" I screamed.

"I didn't mean to."

"What am I going to do?"

"I don't know!"

"I'm going to tell him you threw it."

"I'll lie!"

The clock was ticking. My parents could arrive at any minute. And the Frisbee was clearly visible from the driveway.

What to do? What to do?

Then I was struck by a moment of brilliance. I ran into the garage and brought out one of my fishing poles, which was already rigged with a lure. All I had to do was cast it up there, hook the Frisbee, and reel it back to the ground. No harm, no foul!

My first cast was too short. So was my second. On the third try, I gave it a little more oomph. Too much oomph! The lure flew clear over the roof and landed in the backyard.

I FREAKED OUT AGAIN!

As I reeled like a madman, the lure caught on the backyard rain gutter. I tugged and tugged, but it was hopeless. Even as I attempted to overcome this latest conundrum, I heard one of my friends shout,

"They're coming!"

I turned and looked down the road. Sure enough, my parents' Buick Skylark was only a minute or two away. I let go of the fishing pole, which dangled off the roof of the house, swaying like Poe's pendulum. There was no escape.

Then I uttered two words that would amuse my friends for years to come.

"I'M DOOMED!!!"

My friends took off running, abandoning me to my fate just as my parents pulled into the driveway.

The fishing pole continued to swing back and forth.

Doom was indeed at hand.

In the end, I got lucky. My parents had been at an afternoon cocktail party and were in cheerful moods. Even they had to laugh about the absurdity of it all.

Thankfully, the incident was soon forgotten, but the words "I'M DOOMED!" lived on for what seemed like forever.

THE DIVING BELL

Throughout my childhood in Florida, I spent most of my playtime outdoors. But even a beach boy like me wasn't entirely immune to the heat and humidity, especially during the height of summer. My friend and I weren't complete fools. Sometimes it made more sense to stay indoors during the worst of the afternoon. And from ages 8 through 12, our favorite form of indoor entertainment was playing with our G.I. Joe dolls. We each had more than a dozen of them, and I'm talking the bad-ass Hasbro originals that stood twelve inches tall. You didn't want to tick off one of those dudes.

Our parents were huge fans of G.I. Joes. They kept us out of trouble for hours at a time and were also guaranteed hits for birthdays and Christmases.

A couple of G.I. Joes with some groovy outfits and accessories, and we were good to go.

When I said we played for hours, I meant it. We'd shut the door to his bedroom or mine after lunch and not come out until dinnertime. Our imaginations were limitless. The G.I. Joes became soldiers, astronauts, superheroes, professional wrestlers, adventurers, athletes, and rock musicians. For the latter, our favorite G.I. Joes danced to the tinny music blaring from an aging 45 rpm record player. My friend's biggest hit was *The Night Has a Thousand Eyes* (Bobby Vee). Mine was *Oh, Pretty Woman* (Roy Orbison). We even snuck into our sisters' rooms a few times and "borrowed" their Barbies so that our rock stars could have some female companionship after a raucous concert. (It wasn't as bad as it sounds.)

The original G.I. Joes were impressively durable. You could throw them all over the room and they wouldn't break. We even took them outside. Once, we made parachutes out of cloth and string and heaved our newly commissioned paratroopers high into the air. The parachutes didn't work, but the G.I. Joes survived the falls with only minor external damage.

The rugged dolls had one annoying flaw. Their right hand was shaped like a fist with a thumb sticking out, but the left hand had four extended fingers that could sometimes break off. You knew a G.I. Joe had some age on him if he was missing fingers on his left hand. But my friend and I had a fix for that. The arms twisted off at the elbows and were replaceable, so he and I would occasionally sneak into a nearby department store and steal a left arm from one of the new G.I. Joes on display. We never got caught, but we must have bemused the heck out of the store's employees when customers kept returning to demand left arms for their new toys.

One time, I became obsessed with one of the special G.I. Joe outfits I had gotten for Christmas. The Star Trek-like outfit was blue; I wanted it to be white. Why? Who knows? I had probably seen something I liked on TV. Anyway, I poured an inch of bleach into a garden bucket and soaked the outfit in it. For a couple of days, nothing happened. But when I checked on it one last time, the outfit had finally become dazzling white. Hooray! However, when I scooped it out of the bleach with a screwdriver, the outfit fell apart like wet tissue paper. That was the end of that.

A relative gave my friend another doll (he and I didn't call them dolls, of course) that was like a bargain-basement G.I. Joe, but this doll had one redeeming attribute: He was amazingly flexible. When my friend tossed him around the room, I liked the way that doll flopped when he landed. Without thinking it through, I traded one of my best G.I. Joes for Mr. Floppy. Soon after, I realized how stupid I had been but it was too late to turn back. He became my trash doll. I even used a black marker to draw tattoos all over him.

One day my friend and I found an old metal box in his dad's garage. It was the size of a shoebox, but it had a sturdy latch that held the lid snugly closed. We even sprayed a hose on it and were delighted to find the inside still dry when we opened it. Then an idea came to us. We would conduct a grand experiment. The metal box would become a diving bell that we would rope to the end of my friend's dock and then drop into the water.

All we needed was a volunteer for this bold and dangerous adventure.

Mr. Floppy Tattoo Guy volunteered. (Okay, I volunteered him, if you want to get technical.) We put him inside, added a few rocks for ballast, and tied one end of the rope to a handle on the box. Then we dropped it into the water and watched it sink quickly to the bottom. After tying the other end of the rope to the dock, the underwater experiment began.

For six weeks, we checked on the diving bell every day, sometimes several times a day. The water was too murky and deep to provide a good view of the submerged box, so we mainly visited only to make sure the rope remained intact. Despite being impatient boys, we somehow maintained the discipline to not haul the box up and examine it from time to time. In our minds, this would have ruined the experiment.

Finally the big day arrived. In a dramatic scene televised around the world, we hauled the diving bell to the surface. Other than having a couple of small barnacles on it, the outside remained unmarred. Then came the moment we were all waiting for. We opened the box. To our dismay, the saltwater had found its way inside. Mr. Floppy Tattoo Guy was soaked, shrunken, and sad.

Even after drying him in the hot Florida sun for several days, he never smelled the same. To honor his bravery, we gave him a soldier's burial in one of the sandy fields across the street from our houses.

For all I know, he's still where we left him … fifty-five years ago. Is there such a thing as a plastic skeleton?

INTERLUDE III

Many anglers prize freshwater catfish. They are fun to catch and tasty to eat. Saltwater catfish? Not so much. Though they put up a good fight, they are otherwise a bane to anglers. It's gross to even imagine eating them, and to make matters worse, they have poisonous spines on their dorsal and pectoral fins that can be quite painful if they pierce your flesh. Much to my dismay, three out of every four fish I catch as a boy are saltwater catfish. (Not a single snook among them!) One day something scary happens. I'm fishing off a dock with some friends when one of the boys—who is wearing a pair of boots with thick rubber soles—reels in an especially large catfish. He hates catfish more than any of us, and in a fit of rage, he raises his right foot and smashes it down on the catfish to squash it. Only, just as he does this, the catfish raises its dorsal fin and its spine penetrates all the way through the rubber sole deep into our friend's foot. He screams in agony even as the fish wiggles frenetically to free itself. The boy's dad sees this and races out with pliers and a pair of snips. We hold our friend down as the dad grasps the spine with the pliers and then cuts it off with the snips. Still in terrible pain, my friend is rushed to the emergency room to remove the part of the spine still buried in the tender arch of his foot. This shakes us all up pretty good, and we earn a new respect—and further dislike—for saltwater catfish. We certainly learn never to stomp on one. Holy moly!

THE SPIDER MONKEY

One of my friend's older sisters owned a pet spider monkey who lived in a cage on his family's screened porch. I can't remember the monkey's name, but I remember a lot about him, otherwise.

Being mischievous boys, it was a severe test of our willpower not to tease the monkey. If we tapped on the cage or made monkey sounds, he would get overly excited and jump around and screech. However, we rarely did that—not because we were good boys but because my friend's mom threatened us with death if she ever caught us doing it. And my friend's mom didn't mess around.

Even when not being teased, the monkey was a lot of fun. When we let him out of his cage, he raced around their entire house, leaping from couches to chairs to cabinets with the speed and dexterity of Tarzan on his best day. He would also sit on our shoulders and pick things out of our hair. I hope whatever he found wasn't alive.

I remember a fateful day in late fall of 1969. It was a cool afternoon by Florida standards, with temperatures in the high 60s (rare) and low humidity (rarer). Those kinds of days were a treat and drew people from their homes as if to witness an extraordinary phenomenon of nature. A group of at least thirty adults and kids gathered in my front yard. My mom was there too, and she seemed in an especially good mood. My friend's sister even brought her spider monkey, which was strapped into a small harness attached to a leash.

My mom had heard me tell stories about the monkey, but this was the first time she had seen him face to face. And he immediately charmed her. The monkey also took a liking to my mom, perching on her shoulder as if he had known her his entire life.

This went on for probably half an hour until it

reached the point where my mom half-forgot the monkey was even there. She stood next to some thick bushes in our front yard and carried on a conversation with the neighbors as if it was perfectly natural to do so with a monkey next to her ear.

However, I was keeping a close watch. Boys my age had a sixth sense of when something hilarious might happen, and they didn't want to miss it. As if on cue, the monkey sprang off my mom's shoulder into the bushes, scrambled around a bit, and then pounced back onto her shoulder. In one of his tiny hands he held an enormous lizard, easily eight inches long including its tail. My mom turned her head to look. The monkey held the lizard close enough to her face to graze the tip of her nose. And then he chomped off the lizard's head.

The scream that erupted from my mom's mouth was so piercing and intense, the entire neighborhood stopped in its tracks. The monkey screeched almost as loudly as my mom, then he rushed back to my friend's sister while my mom high-tailed it to our front door.

It was too funny for me to bear. I rolled around on the grass, laughing hard enough to pass out.

Five decades later, I still chuckle whenever this memory pops into my head.

THE DOGS OF COQUINA KEY

In the 1960s, there was no such thing as leash laws (at least that I knew of). Where I lived, everyone let their dogs run free, which was great news for the dogs but not so great for the cats—or sometimes, for kids. It wasn't unusual to be zipping down the road on your bike and get attacked by a snarling dog. No problem. We kicked the dog in the snout and kept on pedaling. Whatever.

My dog was a seventy-pound purebred standard poodle named Sam. Though standard poodles are renowned for their intelligence, it pains me to say that Sam was an exception to the rule. He was friendly and adorable, but he was also dumb as a box of rocks—and a coward to boot. I loved him, anyway.

Sam had a bad habit that often got him—and my

family—in trouble. For some crazy reason, he loved to sneak up behind women and goose their rear ends with his wet nose, especially if they were wearing skirts. He once did this to the wife of one of our neighbors when she was on her hands and knees weeding her garden. She screamed as if death were upon her, which enraged her 6-foot-6 husband. The snarling giant thundered over to our house and confronted my stepdad, who was 5-foot-7 on his best day. Luckily, the man didn't kill my stepdad, but for a moment there, I thought for sure he would.

My friend down the road had a dog named King who was the opposite of Sam. King was the quintessential mutt, and like a lot of mutts, he was smart. For his relatively diminutive size (about 30 pounds), he was also one tough sombeech.

While Sam was a gorgeous dog with silky black fur that didn't shed, King was one of those mangy-looking dogs whose fangs protruded from the bottom of his mouth instead of the top. Sam was more than twice King's size, but it was clear who was the boss. King would rise on his hind legs, place his front paws on Sam's back, and growl menacingly. Sam would stand there looking happy as can be, his tongue lolling goofily. They never fought, but only because Sam never gave King a reason.

Though Sam roamed free, he rarely wandered far. King, on the other hand, was an adventurer. No, check that. He was a pirate! And he sailed the seven seas of Coquina Key with a free rein. King was also renowned as a canine Casanova. I'm sure there were many people who wondered why there were so many puppies on the island with upside-down fangs. It must be a dominant gene.

After Sam passed away, my family purchased a ten-pound silky terrier named Susie Q who turned out to be a lot like Sam. She was gorgeous but also exceedingly dumb. Susie Q's claim to fame was an obsession with a red rubber ball about the size of a racquetball. From early morning until late at night, Susie Q would chase that ball all over hell's half acre. My family, friends, and anyone else who came to visit grew accustomed to it. While we sat in the living room having a chat, Susie Q would drop her ball in one of our laps. We'd toss it. She'd chase it. We'd toss it. She'd chase it. We'd toss it. She'd chase it. I could copy and paste this a thousand times and not approach her proclivity. Susie Q was so obsessed with the ball, if it fell into the pool she would leap in and swim to the bottom to retrieve it, even in the deep end. If one of us was swimming underwater and surfaced by the side of the pool, Susie Q would be there, dropping the ball next to us with the frenzied hope that we would throw it. She would then chase after it so fast, the pads of her paws would bleed on the pool deck.

Susie Q had another loony habit. She liked to evacuate her bowels in the short hallway that led from my parents' bedroom to their master bathroom. On many a dark night, my stepdad would make his way to the bathroom in his bare feet only to let loose a string of profanities ribald enough to shame the devil. As you might imagine by now, I would lie in bed and laugh myself silly. One time it happened twice in one night, and I was lucky to survive the heart-pounding theatrics of my hysterically explosive reaction.

Sam, King, and Susie Q were only the tip of the iceberg of the Dogs of Coquina Key. A German Shepherd (coincidentally named King) and a Doberman Pinscher named Lodi engaged in epic battles that would make Godzilla versus King Kong pale in comparison. These two were the unquestioned titans of our neighborhood.

Both lived across the street from where I lived, two enormous dogs in adjacent houses. Lodi weighed about 90 pounds, King 100-plus. And to make matters worse, the two behemoths did not like each other.

When I was 12, I babysat for Lodi's owners whose two kids were then 4 and 5. (It blows my mind to think those kids are now about 60 years old.) Anyway, I remember the kids as being good-natured and well-behaved, so it was an easy way to earn some money. But Lodi was another story. He would follow me around the house, keeping a close eye on everything I did. When I went to the bathroom, I had to shut the door quickly just to have some privacy. I wasn't about to relieve my bladder with those jaws only a few inches away from you know what. And when I sat on their couch and watched TV with the kids, he loomed in front of me and stared with an expression that was like: *Should I kill this evil stranger or let him live? I'm leaning toward the former.* It would be an understatement to say this made me a little nervous, but I somehow survived with all my parts intact.

One day a bunch of us were playing in the street, and King (the mutt, not the German Shepherd) trotted up, saw Lodi, and challenged the Doberman to a fight. King the mutt imagined himself a tough guy, but it quickly became clear that he was way out of his league. Lodi didn't hurt King in any significant way, but he disabled him as efficiently as a highly trained martial artist, biting King by the scruff of his neck and holding on tight. The smaller dog realized he had made a serious mistake and howled pathetically. And though he was a weakling compared to Lodi, he still dragged the larger dog several hundred feet down the road. My friends and

I chased after them, hollering like madmen. King eventually wrestled free and headed for the hills while Lodi simply trotted confidently back to his own home.

The German Shepherd version of King was not such a pushover. You might find this difficult to believe, but I once saw him get run over by a fair-sized pickup truck and jump up none the worse for wear. His ribcage must have been forged from steel. I rushed to King, expecting to find him half-dead, but he simply wagged his tail and licked me on the face. His owners didn't even have to take him to the vet. Meanwhile, the driver of the truck zoomed off. It was a hit and run. We never found out who did it, but King didn't seem to care.

On a breezy evening in late spring, the legendary Fight of the Century took place in front of my house. King was running around with us kids when Lodi somehow got outside. The two dogs went nose to nose. At first it looked like it might end in a standoff, then both dogs tore into each other. It was so scary, none of us dared approach.

Lodi's owner heard the ruckus and ran outside. Then he amazed us by leaping onto King's back in an attempt to separate the snarling canines, but it was an impossible task. No matter what he did, the dogs continued to fight, and he was thrown to the ground like a rag doll.

One of my friends banged on the door of the house where King lived. His owner came out, quickly unwound his garden hose, and sprayed the dogs. This separated them enough to buy time for the two men to drag each dog inside their respective houses.

The fight was over. There was no clear winner. Even better, there was no clear loser.

Eventually, both families moved away. I heard nothing more about Lodi and King. When the titans were gone the axis of power shifted and the mutt-sized version of King took over as lord of the neighborhood. My dog Sam had no issue with that.

GATORS, ROACHES AND MORE

My friends and I played football in a large grassy field at Lake Maggiore Park in St. Petersburg. Back then, the lake wasn't what I would consider a thing of beauty. It was broad but not deep, and several feet of disgusting muck smothered its once-sandy bottom. That was a good reason not to swim in it. But there was an even better one.

Alligators

The lake was full of them. It wasn't uncommon for a 10-foot alligator to sun itself on the bank less than a stone's throw from where we were unleashing violent tackles and scoring dramatic touchdowns.

Most bodies of freshwater in Florida had alligators. The behemoths even found their way into our swimming pools. I can't claim to have had any dramatic encounters, but I would occasionally walk over to one just to see how close I could get before it scrambled into the water. It barely entered my mind that it might charge toward me. Besides, I had speed to burn.

Anyone who has spent time in Florida has seen alligators. And if you lived there long enough, you saw them every day at one place or another.

Are there people in the world who have never seen an alligator in person? To a Florida boy like me, that seemed impossible to believe.

There are other commonplace things in Florida that might not be as common to people who have never visited the state. Here are a few examples:

Lizards

A variety of lizards thrives in Florida (you'll read more about his in Interlude IV). But the ones I grew up with were mostly green and brown anoles. During daylight hours, anoles were as common as flies (their favorite food). I could stroll around the outside of my house and count thirty or more, and those were only the ones that were easily visible. More likely, my backyard was home to hundreds.

I was a boy. And boys like to do boy things. My friends and I would catch a couple of big lizards, dangle them by their tails over a bucket, bang their heads together, and drop them into the bucket. The feisty lizards would fight like dinosaurs. Was this cruel? Of course! And I wouldn't do such a thing now. Back then, it was another way to pass the time.

Seagulls

Everyone has seen a seagull, right? There are over fifty different species found around the world. In Florida, the most numerous species was herring gulls—and they were everywhere! In oceans, seas, lakes, ponds, McDonald's parking lots (they loved French fries and just about anything that was even remotely edible). If you were at the beach eating potato chips, watch out! They would swoop down and snatch a chip out of your fingers, onion dip and all.

In my late teens, I worked at a seafood restaurant

located inside a marina (more on this later). The marina held a yearly fishing tournament called the Suncoast Tarpon Roundup. Back then, there was no such thing as catch-and-release. Contestants would bring in dead tarpon to be weighed and measured, and since tarpon weren't edible, the organizers of the roundup would simply fling hundreds of them into iron dumpsters that stood side by side across the street from the restaurant. It took a couple of days before the dumpsters were emptied. Meanwhile, the horrific odor of rotting tarpon would attract rats the size of beer cans. The rats then attracted seagulls, which swallowed the vermin whole. What a way to go, huh?

(Did you know that seagulls can devour fully grown squirrels?)

Great blue herons

In my current home in the mountains of Upstate South Carolina, I occasionally see a great blue heron, but in Florida I saw them all the time. Because of their long necks and legs, they stood almost five feet tall with a seven-foot wingspan. Yet they were unerringly graceful and hunted their prey with hypnotic precision. Blue herons weren't as numerous as seagulls, of course, but I hardly went a day without stopping to watch one artfully snare a fish with its pointy beak.

Bald eagles

It also wasn't unusual to see bald eagles. The majestic birds would swoop down to the surface of the water only a hundred feet from the seawall in my backyard and pluck a wriggling mullet out of the bay. If out-of-town guests were at our house and saw this, they would shout in amazement. I was so used to it I couldn't understand what the fuss was about.

Mosquitoes

For every bald eagle, there were twenty blue herons. For every blue heron, there were 100 alligators. For every alligator, there were 1,000 seagulls. And for every seagull, there were 1,000,000,000,000,000 mosquitoes. And these suckers were bad asses. In the summer, I could barely go outside in the evening, especially around dusk. Florida mosquitoes were angry at the world.

Cockroaches

These hideous insects weren't as numerous as mosquitoes, but a day hardly passed when I didn't have to squash at least a couple of them inside our house. This was the main reason mothers in Florida liked to have sons. We were the designated cockroach smashers.

Like the mosquitoes, Florida cockroaches (especially the Palmetto bug version) were massive and fearless. There were a lot of terrifying things in life—and having a 4-inch-long Palmetto bug run up your bare leg was certainly one of them.

Fire ants

For such a tiny insect, fire ants packed a powerful punch. Where I lived, they were everywhere. And all of us hated them.

I remember taking a swim in my family pool on a broiling summer day. There had been no rain in more than a week, so a refreshing dip was just what

I needed. When I climbed out of the pool and stood on the deck, I noticed a fire-ant mound in the grass about ten feet away. My first thought was how to dispose of the ants—mercilessly—and I came up with the brilliant idea of dousing the mound with gasoline and then setting it on fire. I marched into our garage and got the gas tank we used for the lawnmower, snatched a pack of matches, and went to war. I poured several cups of gas on the mound, lit a match, and dropped it on the mound. Poof! It burst into flame, surely destroying every ant in the mound. Mission accomplished!

Only, not quite.

The grass surrounding the mound had gone brown from the lack of rain, and it caught fire, slowly at first, but then expanding until it suddenly seemed that I was about to burn down our house and the entire neighborhood along with it. The only thing I could think to do was grab my diving mask, dip it into the pool and fill it with a few ounces of water, then rush over and splash it on the fire. Even though I was running back and forth with the superhero speed of The Flash, the fire spread faster and faster, now encompassing half the backyard.

Luckily for me, my parents had hired a handyman to make some improvements in our kitchen, and he hustled out of the house carrying a pair of thick towels which he soaked in the pool and then tossed on the fire. Our combined efforts finally extinguished the blaze. Afterward, he laughed his head off—and I laughed too.

But as funny as it turned out to be, my hatred for fire ants will never be extinguished.

Palm trees

Almost every yard in Florida has a palm tree or two or ten. In fact, Florida has more palm trees than any other state.

Whenever I return to visit, it stuns me how many palm trees there are. But as a boy, I wasn't a big fan because they weren't much fun to climb, making them useless to me. Plus, they shed palm fronds all over the yard and driveway. And guess who was the designated palm-frond picker-upper.

Sandspurs

In terms of sheer numbers, sandspurs might rank number two to mosquitoes. Avoiding them was impossible. If I had a nickel for every time I stepped barefoot on a sandspur, I would be rich beyond measure. If they got into your yard, one plant could become a dozen in less than a week. They were the spiky scourge of my boyhood, and I hate them with a passion to this day. At least, there are no sandspurs in the mountains where I live now.

Afternoon thunderstorms

With climate change screwing up weather patterns, I don't know if it's still this way in Florida, but when I was a boy it rained every afternoon around 4 o'clock, especially in the summer.

In only a few minutes, the sky changed from light blue to nearly black. Stupendous bolts of lightning crashed upon the land. Forty mile-per-hour winds lashed the palm trees, scared the lizards, and scattered the mosquitoes. Even the seagulls went into hiding. I'm not sure what the alligators and cockroaches did.

An inch of rain could fall in fifteen minutes. And as quickly as it began, the storm passed, the sky became blue again, the heat returned, steam rose from the streets, and life went on as before.

Heat/humidity

To say that Florida is hot and humid is like saying that Mount Everest is tall. When I was a boy, it rarely got much above 92 degrees, but the humidity was also 92, which made the feel-like temperature hover around 184. And that wasn't the worst part. It sometimes reached the low 90s as early as March or as late as November. It wasn't unheard of to run around outdoors in shorts and a T-shirt on Christmas Day.

Did it ever snow? Ha!!!!!!!!!!!!!!! 🤣

Sunburns

I had probably fifty sunburns between the ages of 5 and 18, which is the reason I now go to a dermatologist twice a year and face the terror of the liquid nitrogen gun. But as much as the gun hurts, it's not nearly as bad as stepping on a sandspur.

Back then, everyone believed in getting a "healthy tan." Not so much anymore, which is one reason I no longer live in Florida. I traded seas for lakes, beaches for hiking trails, palm trees for tulip poplars, and 92 degrees for 72 degrees.

But even up here, I never forget to cover my retired-dude bald spot with a hat.

INTERLUDE IV

When my stepdad's mom dies, it falls to me to go to her house and do some cleaning, which includes disposing of a four-foot-tall pile of carpeting that has lain in her carport for years and gone rancid. The damp and moldy carpet is swarming with cockroaches, and as I scoop up heavy piles of the torn and sodden rug with a pitchfork and heave them into a dumpster, the cockroaches scatter everywhere. Within seconds, an army of lizards appears and revels in the feast of a lifetime. One of the smaller lizards somehow devours a cockroach that looks even bigger than he. I still remember it like it was yesterday. The moral of this story? Humans hate cockroaches, but lizards can't get enough of them.

SAFETY PATROL

In sixth grade I became a member of the Safety Patrol at Lakewood Elementary, one of only a handful of top students who received this honor. I wanted it bad for a long time, so it thrilled me to get it. Members of the Safety Patrol wore orange belts that looped over their shoulders and snapped around their waists. So cool! The only negative was that we had to arrive at school an hour before the bell rang each morning, but this was only a minor inconvenience to a kid like me who typically woke up early. (Nowadays, I can barely haul myself out of bed before 9.)

Each week, the administrators gave us a different assignment. The primo job was street duty, which the Safety Patrol held with utmost regard. We helped students cross the street and kept them safe from traffic. When we said go, they went—and vice versa. Even the bratty first-graders respected the Safety Patrol. We were the cream of the crop.

When not assigned to street duty, I performed other tasks that varied in interest and importance. One of the most boring ones was guarding a glass door at the rear of the school. It was my job to stop anyone from entering or exiting the school through the door without permission. The problem was that no one ever tried, so I stood there bored out of my mind until the bell rang and set me free.

(Keep in mind this was 1968. In the twenty-first century, I highly doubt any school would assign a sixth-grade student to be the lone guard at an entry point where a shooter armed with an AR-15-style rifle might approach. Most all school doors are now locked and armed with security cameras and alarms. Back then, it crossed no one's mind that there was anything dangerous about guarding a school door.)

One task I enjoyed almost as much as street duty was manning the outdoor water fountain in the recess area where kids gathered before the start of the school day. I had god-like powers over the fountain, allowing kids to drink for only about five seconds before cutting off their water supply. Some kids would have stood there and slurped all morning if I had let them, but I ruled with an iron fist. No exceptions. Gulp fast and make room for the next person!

After the first bell rang, I shut off all drinking privileges. The students knew it was time to form lines, and stopping to take a drink would have messed things up. No kid, no matter how large, would have dared challenge me on this. The orange Safety Patrol belt was a talisman that wielded unquestionable power.

I was known as one of the "good kids" at school, mostly because I liked school but also because I had a healthy fear of the wrath of teachers and administrators. However, one morning when I was on duty at the water fountain, something odd came over me. In a fit of uncharacteristic misbehavior, I sprayed some kids standing nearest the fountain by holding my thumb partially over the spout, creating enough pressure to shoot a geyser of water twenty feet or more. The kids ducked and screamed, but it was all in good fun because it was a warm enough morning to make the cool water feel refreshing. It wasn't like it took long to dry off! Soon everyone was laughing and cheering, including me.

Until ……

A teacher strode over to me and shouted, "What do you think you're doing!?"

Everyone went silent.

"Sorry …" I mumbled.

The teacher gave me a stern look.

"James! I never want to see you do that again."

I lowered my head, filled with good-kid shame.

"Yes ma'am."

After the quick tongue-lashing, the teacher let me off the hook. Like most first-time offenders, I got off easy. But they never assigned me water-fountain duty again.

THE TOAD

When I was in seventh grade, my science teacher announced one Friday that when we came back to class on Monday we would dissect toads. The boys cheered. The girls feigned disgust. Or so I remember it.

There was a caveat. We were told in no uncertain terms that our weekend assignment was to catch a toad and bring it to class so we would each have one to dissect. Not doing this without a good excuse would lower our grade.

Where I grew up, a student began receiving letter grades in fourth grade. Since that first fateful report card, I had been a nearly straight-A student. There was an occasional B but *never* a C, though my good grades were less about my intelligence and more about studying hard and always doing my homework—which on this weekend included capturing a toad. Per usual, I took the assignment seriously.

Not wanting to force a toad to be trapped in a cardboard box longer than necessary, I waited until Sunday evening to go on the hunt. There were plenty of toads in Florida, so I knew I would succeed. It was just a matter of when and where. After sniffing around the yard for a while, I found a big one hiding in tall grass next to our air conditioning unit. When I picked up the toad, it peed on my hands. But I was a boy accustomed to disgusting things, so this didn't deter me. Into the box it went, trembling in terror but unaware that worse was yet to come. The toad was destined to meet its doom in the grisliest way possible.

During the bus ride to school the next morning, several friends asked me what I had in the box. I opened the lid and showed them the toad. A couple of kids were in my same science class. I asked them about their toads. None of them had brought one.

"But it'll lower your grade," I said.

"I doubt it," one of them responded. "Mrs. (I can't remember her name) is always saying stuff like that, but she never really does anything."

This perplexed me. Had I gone to all this trouble for nothing? And even worse, I was feeling more and more sorry for the toad. What had he (or she) ever done to me to deserve such a fate? Every time I looked in the box, the toad stared back at me forlornly.

Sure enough, I was the only one to bring a toad to science class. Not a single other kid brought so much as a cricket. Now I was really feeling weird. A part of me wanted to race out of the classroom with the toad in tow and set it free in the bushes outside school.

But no. Our teacher had him now, and though she seemed ticked off that there was only one toad to dissect, she probably figured one was better than none. Then she described how to quickly and mercifully kill a toad. You take a needle, jam it through the top of its skull, wiggle the needle around, and scramble the toad's brains. Simple Simon.

As she was driving the needle through the top of his head, the toad looked directly at me. This was not my imagination. The toad looked *directly at me*! And his expression said: "How can you allow this to happen? I thought we were friends! Arrrggghhhh. It hurts. Arrrggghhhh. *I'M GOING TO DIE ... PLEASE SAVE ME*!!!"

Our teacher was wrong about both the quick and the merciful parts. The poor thing squirmed for what seemed like an hour. It was more like two minutes, but two minutes is a lot longer than a few seconds, which is how I would define quick and merciful.

When the toad was finally dead, our teacher asked me if I wanted to be the one to dissect it since I had been the only student (STUPID ENOUGH!) to bring a toad to class. By this point, I was sick to my stomach and declined her offer, as did every other kid. In the end, our teacher performed the butchery while we watched. I now was an accessory to murder and deserved nothing less than life in prison. Maybe even the electric chair.

There was one minor consolation. This time, our

teacher lived up to her word. I was the only kid to get an A for the assignment, but it was a high price to pay. I mourned the toad's death for months and even had a couple of nightmares about its gruesome demise.

As I write this, I'm a retired dude far removed from seventh grade, yet the wretched experience still weighs on my mind. If there is such a thing as life after death, I can only hope that an army of vengeful toads wielding wicked needles isn't waiting for me on the other side.

ALL MY JOBS

Like most people, I can be accused of a lot of things, but laziness isn't one of them. Before my recent retirement, I worked long hours at stressful jobs for more than four decades. Many people can say the same, but for the majority of them the demanding jobs started when they became adults. For me, they began when I was 12 years old.

Mowing lawns at 100 pounds (ages 12-13)

I was 5 feet 4 and weighed 100 pounds soaking wet. However, I was athletic for a kid my size and always hyper-eager to prove to people that being skinny didn't mean I was a weakling.

A woman who recently had lost her husband lived a few houses down from mine, and one day she asked me if I could mow her lawn and offered $2.50. I jumped at the opportunity. Back then, that kind of money could buy enough sodas and snacks to last a week.

The word spread. Soon I had a second customer and then a third. My friend who lived down the road joined me. He was a year older and quite a bit bigger, so he helped our burgeoning operation pass the eye test.

Back then, Coquina Key had a popular little weekly newspaper that was distributed to everyone on the island. It reported news of huge importance, like someone's rowboat had sunk or the local Little General convenience store was expanding its parking lot. The newspaper also had a page of advertisements, including kids who mowed lawns. My friend and I joined the list. At first, we were the last of ten. Two years later, we were at the top, the Kings of Coquina Key lawnmower dudes.

During the school year, we mowed lawns after school and on weekends. In the summer, we mowed lawns pretty much seven days a week. Overall, we mowed hundreds and hundreds of lawns. For kids our age, we had lots of money. My bony body might not have been a chick magnet, but my fat wallet was.

I averaged $20 a week.

Cleaning movie theaters in the middle of the night (age 14)

During one long summer, I worked for a janitorial service that cleaned the Plaza Movie Theaters and other businesses in St. Petersburg in the middle of the night. More times than I would have preferred, the two men who ran the business left me alone in the theaters while they drove away to knock off another job. Being by myself in a massive movie theater at 3 in the morning was the stuff of nightmares for a 14-year-old, especially when the theater was showing horror flicks and there were posters of vampires and werewolves plastered all over the place. As I walked along each aisle picking up empty boxes of popcorn and candy, I would swear that I saw something rise from behind a seat out of the corner of my eye. It scared the crap out of me and made me want to shag ass out of there.

The good news was that I usually found a couple dollars' worth of change on the floor, which I adeptly pocketed. I once found a wallet with more than $400 in it, but as the sun rose while I was polishing the glass doors and windows at the front of the theater, a panicked man rushed from the parking lot and laid claim to it. Oh well, I wouldn't have felt good keeping it (I suppose).

Sometimes, I worked all night and then continued until noon the following day because the janitorial service would pick up an extra job such as cleaning debris around a new house under construction. I still remember sitting in breathless heat in the empty bathtub of a house under construction delicately scraping droplets of paint off the acrylic surface with a razor blade.

This was the only job I've ever had where I worked all night and slept during the day. It was weird.

I made $1.65 an hour, not including the money I found in the theaters.

Frying chicken and burning my thumb (age 15)

I worked for most of the year at a fried chicken restaurant called Chicken Unlimited. The place was damn popular and sold a lot of chicken. I became the best fryer on staff, and like a car mechanic who reeks of motor oil, I smelled like fried chicken at the end of each shift even after a hot shower.

On the Fourth of July, a couple of people called in sick, leaving only the manager and me to staff the entire restaurant. I ended up working from noon until past midnight during which there was a perennial line of customers at least ten-deep. It would have gone on even longer, but my stepdad finally showed up and gave the manager hell for making me work such long hours.

Another time, I was scraping debris off the sides of the fryer when my right thumb accidentally slipped into the searing grease, causing me to howl in pain. A co-worker rushed to me with a cup of ice water. As soon as I put my thumb in the frigid water, the pain went away, but if I took my thumb out, the torment returned with a vengeance. Several hours later when I was back home, I took my thumb out of the cup for good and lay in bed with tears in my eyes until the agony finally subsided. At least I didn't suffer any permanent damage.

Not long after that, I gave up frying chicken.

I made $2.65 an hour.

The seafood restaurant: work, exercise, homework (ages 16-20)

My next job was busboy at a seafood restaurant called Seaman's Cove, which was on the waterfront within a thriving marina. The restaurant was extremely popular—and like most busy restaurants, it was especially crazy Friday through Sunday. A German couple owned and operated Seaman's Cove. They were a little grumpy but treated their employees well enough.

My job was to clear tables, and I became a champion at it. I could lift ten water glasses—five in each hand, one in each finger—at once. I could clear a table, wipe it down, and then set up napkins, silverware, and fresh glasses of water in about five minutes flat. The servers loved me. My lawnmower friend had started working there before me and he helped me get the job. Many nights it became a competition between the two of us as to who could clear the most tables during the rush hours. To this day, both of us would claim superiority.

Meanwhile, the owners toyed with the idea of having a valet service. Parking was at a premium, so restaurant customers had to park all over the place, blocking driveways and annoying the people who lived on their boats in the marina.

Across the street from the restaurant was an enormous dry-stack storage building that held over a hundred boats. It was four stories tall and as wide as a warehouse. Behind the building was a parking lot that was too far away for customers to park but not too far for a teenage boy who could run like the wind.

Another friend, who was also a busboy, became the restaurant's first valet, sitting at a card table out front. It started out slow, but customers caught on and started using the service. The restaurant offered it for free, but most people tipped 50 cents or even a dollar. Eventually my friend took another job, giving me the opportunity to become the next valet. I was 17, and it turned out to be my last job before graduating from college. In fact, it helped pay for most of my college education (which was much more affordable back then) with some spending money left over.

I loved being a valet because it killed three birds with one stone: 1) it was my job; 2) I got tons of exercise running back and forth from the restaurant to the parking lot; 3) during slow periods, I sat at the card table and did most of my homework.

Here's how it worked. A customer would drive up, give me his keys, and enter the restaurant. I would then park the car behind the dry-stack building. When the customer came out to leave, I would run more than the length of a football field to get the car and return it to the customer. Over the months, all the running worked me into terrific shape. To be honest, I became one of the fastest men in the world. My exploits were legendary. I was like Forrest Gump with brains. Watching me run became a highlight for Seaman's Cove customers. I also made a lot of money in tips—probably far more, even, than the owners realized. If they had known how much I made, they might have wanted some of it back.

Another perk of the job was that I got to drive every make and model of car imaginable—from Corvette Stingrays (which I covet to this day) to Rolls-Royces (which I also covet to this day).

Speaking of Rolls-Royces, I was a stickler for not allowing customers to park in non-designated areas, but I made an exception for a rich guy who drove a gorgeous Rolls-Royce the color of Dom Pérignon. He looked to be in his 50s and his wife—who wore skirts so short I had to turn my head away when she was getting out of the car—was in her late 20s. None of that mattered to me. All I cared about was that the rich guy tipped me $20 to park his car in a special place where it couldn't get dinged. And I did this greedily. Keep in mind that $20 in the 1970s was equivalent to over $100 now.

I graduated high school at age 17 and college at

20 with a bachelor's degree in journalism. Soon after, I quit the valet job and began my first true career, becoming an award-winning journalist for the next thirty-five years.

But from age 12 until 20, it was quite a run—both literally and figuratively.

(Oh, in case you're wondering, I averaged about $250 a week as a valet. I was rollin' in it, baby!)

INTERLUDE V

The game is on. It's 9:30 on a warm fall evening a couple of days before Halloween. Five of us sneak into a neighbor's yard and creep toward the front door like lions on the prowl. It's dark and oh so quiet. The slightest misstep will give us away. Our goal? To ring the doorbell and run like hell. Then we'll watch from a hiding place in the distance and giggle hysterically when the owners answer the door and look around in confusion. This house is our favorite. It has a large alcove in the front that makes it especially challenging to reach the door unseen. We've rung this doorbell probably a dozen times over the past few months and realize we are pushing our luck. But we can't resist. Only, this time we do not escape unscathed. A menacing figure dressed all in black rises from behind a row of bushes. It hisses, revealing a daunting set of fangs.

Blood drips from the corners of its mouth. A vampire is upon us. "Good eeeevening," it says menacingly, sounding like Bela Lugosi on his most frightening night.

We scream in unison and run like the wind, racing toward the safety of our homes. As you might imagine, we never ring that doorbell again (and I'm sure the dad who pulled the trick on us giggled even harder than we ever did).

THE ULTIMATE DROP

As mentioned in earlier chapters, my friends and I were ultra-competitive. Each of us strove to be faster, stronger, smarter, and braver. Admittedly, I was among the most competitive, to the point of sometimes being obnoxious.

One of our favorite activities was climbing trees. We were fearless, ascending fifty feet or higher without concern. As an adult, I developed a mild fear of heights, but during the ages of 8 through 15, it never entered my mind that climbing trees could be dangerous.

We scooted up pine trees with the dexterity of monkeys and sat there for long stretches, relishing the warm breezes on our faces and enjoying the view. I don't know how many trees I clambered up back then. Hundreds, most likely. But now, I wouldn't attempt any of them.

One of my friends had an enormous oak tree in his backyard. Oaks and many other hardwoods were easier to climb than pines because of their low-lying branches. Pines were sort of like barbershop poles and could be quite challenging.

We spent a lot of time in the friend's oak tree, sitting there and talking while drinking sodas. (We called it soda, not pop.) And as we got older, it was the perfect place to sneak a cigarette. In the 1960s and '70s, most teenagers I knew smoked. Luckily, I quit when I turned 20 and never picked up a cigarette again.

Anyway, here's where our competitiveness kicked in. One of our many dares was to hang by our hands from a branch and then drop onto the sandy earth. This tree had four drops: an easy one, maybe five feet from the soles of our sneakers to the ground; a medium one about eight feet; a difficult one about twelve feet; and an impossible one, which was easily twenty feet.

Everyone could do the first two, and most of us managed the third, though it sometimes resulted in mildly sprained ankles. But the fourth one, the twenty-footer, was beyond all of us. We'd hang there for minutes at a time, attempting to work up the courage to drop, but eventually we'd climb back into the safety of the tree. It was just too scary.

We named it **THE ULTIMATE DROP**. And that name stuck, becoming legendary throughout the island. Many brave souls attempted The Ultimate Drop, but none ever let go of the branch.

Eventually, we gave up.

However ... there was one boy who was on the small side but who bore the heart of a lion. Few of us wanted to fight him, not because he was physically stronger but because he could get mean as a wet hornet. If you got into a fight with him, you would have to knock him unconscious to declare victory. He wouldn't quit unless you made him quit. He reminded me of the famous Mark Twain quote: "It's not the size of the dog in the fight, it's the size of the fight in the dog."

The Ultimate Drop had been a familiar part of my life for years. I had witnessed dozens of boys, including me, chicken out. One day a few of us were up in the tree when the tough boy wandered by and climbed up with us. He seemed in a good mood, so we didn't push our luck. After a few minutes, I told him the larger-than-life story of The Ultimate Drop.

He listened with intense interest—and then, without hesitation, he climbed out onto the branch, hung there for a second, and dropped. Just like that. Then he stood and dusted himself off, apparently no worse for wear.

Our jaws dropped in unison. It was like watching someone break a record most believed untouchable, like Joe DiMaggio's 56-game hitting streak.

I'll never forget it.

And I spent a long time afterward relieved I had never gotten into a fight with that kid.

CATCH OF A LIFETIME

Some of the best memories of my boyhood occurred during a three-year period from ages 10 to 12 when I played Little League Baseball. In my final year, I was one of the five best players on the team. I couldn't hit for power, but I drilled line-drive singles to keep an inning alive. I was also a solid outfielder.

While reading this book, you've probably noticed that my parents have played a minor role in a lot of these stories. To fill in a little more history, my mom and stepdad raised me, and I have one sister who's four years older than me. Because of that age difference, my sister and I rarely hung out together when I was a kid. My parents, including my biological father, are now deceased, but my sister is still going strong, and she and I have a great relationship.

Anyway, my mom was an easygoing person, but my stepdad had quite a temper. He wasn't the physical type. His temper was more just about yelling a lot. Both my parents were heavy drinkers, which led to terrible late-night arguments that were scary to a young kid. I used to lie in bed and listen to them yell at each other, wishing they would stop. And so my boyhood wasn't entirely idyllic. Many people had it worse, some had it better.

I only mention this now to add some context to this chapter. My parents weren't involved much in my life outside of the house. For instance, the Little League complex where I played all my games was about four miles from home. Most of the time, I went back and forth to games and practices on my bike, often pedaling home in the dark. Nowadays, most parents couldn't imagine allowing a 10-year-old boy to ride that far in the dark by himself, but back then it was a common practice in a lot of households.

My parents rarely attended my games—maybe half a dozen in all. And my stepdad was not the volunteer-to-be-coach kind of parent. He was more of a cocktail party kind of guy. Do I sound bitter? I suppose I am. Or maybe just sad.

When I was 12 and in my final year of Little League, my team's coach *was* a volunteer-to-be-coach kind of parent. Two of his sons played for our team, and they were also our two best players. But Coach was a father figure to all of us—kind, patient, and fun to be around. He always encouraged, never yelled. We weren't the best team, but he was the best coach.

One day after a practice when everyone had left except for me and Coach and his sons, he volunteered to give me a little one-on-one instruction. Older teens also used the field we played on, so the outfield fences were about 320 feet from home plate as opposed to a typical Little League field where the fences were more like 200 feet away. Because of this, I could go way out in left field. Coach started hitting some high fly balls that came my way a lot farther and faster than a 12-year-old could ever hit, and at first I struggled. But Coach kept at it, and within thirty minutes I was catching most of them. After about an hour we called it quits, but in that relatively short time, my confidence as an outfielder took a giant leap.

The next evening, our team played the best team in the league, led by a terrific home run hitter who was already muscular at age 12. Surprisingly, we entered the bottom of the sixth inning ahead by one run. (We only played six-inning games at that age.) There was one out, but they had a runner on first base and up to the plate came the superstar. The odds weren't in our favor.

On the first pitch, the larger-than-life boy cranked a stupendous blast to deep left field. In the first fraction of a second, I stepped in the wrong direction, but then my new muscle-memory—honed during my practice session with the coach—kicked in, and I turned and chased after the towering drive. Knowing how good the hitter was, I was already playing deep, but this blast was titanic, not long enough to clear the fence but darn close. Plus, it was moving like a blistering bullet. With all my speed and strength, I ran and then took a giant leap, extending my glove as high in the air as possible. Somehow, I caught the ball.

The small crowd watching the game roared. And amid the hoopla, I heard my coach yell, "GREAT CATCH, SON!!!"

The runner who had been on first base was already rounding third, convinced there was no way that anyone could run that ball down. This forced him to turn and begin the long race back to first. I had a powerful arm for a kid my size, but I also had a habit of occasionally throwing the ball too high. I heaved the ball toward first base as hard as I could. And though the throw had the distance, it leaped toward the heavens like a rocket. I still remember seeing the people in the bleachers looking up at the ball and watching it descend as if they were observing a meteorite fall from the sky.

As the ball spun toward Earth, the boy rounded second and rushed toward first base in a desperate attempt to avoid a game-ending double play. Our first baseman—one of the coach's two sons—waited with glove held high.

Amazingly, the ball dropped into the web of his glove as softly as a fluttering leaf, beating the runner by three steps.

Double play.

Game over.

Victory!

For such a small gathering, there was an explosion of cheers. My teammates and I jumped around like we had won the World Series, clapping each other on the back and howling like loons.

For a day, at least, I was a hero.

GREAT CATCH, SON!!!

Thanks, Coach. For everything.

UP, UP AND AWAY!

When I was a boy, Coquina Key was different than it is now, especially along the waterfront. The interior of the island contained mostly humble two- and three-bedroom homes and even most of the waterfront homes that overlooked Tampa Bay were relatively modest. Our house on the water had four bedrooms and two baths squeezed into 1600 square feet.

More recently, McMansions now occupy the once-empty waterfront lots, and hungry developers have plowed over and replaced some of the original waterfront homes. At least, it was that way the last time I visited the island, which was ten years ago.

In the Sixties, Coquina Key had a lot of undeveloped spaces, including a small forest that covered maybe ten acres; and of course, lots of sandy fields. Kids took advantage of the forest and the fields, where many a first kiss (and slightly beyond) took place.

However, we didn't just play on the ground or in the trees. We also looked to the sky. One of the many advantages of having open spaces was that you could fly things without worrying about landing on someone's roof (except for Frisbees) or getting tangled in a power line. I used to love the rubberband-propelled balsa airplanes. With the right breeze, those lightweight planes could soar several hundred feet. However, I was never one to be satisfied with the way things were designed to operate. Rather than use one rubberband to fly my airplane, I would loop in four thick ones and then wind the propeller so tight you could play the rubberbands like a banjo. I remember launching one of my super-powered airplanes and watching it fly out over the bay, then crash-land deep in the channel. Oops!

I was also obsessed with Estes rockets. That company first opened in the late 1950s and is still going strong today. You could buy a variety of rocket kits, though they weren't as fancy as what they offer nowadays. Back then, the rockets and the engines that powered them came in different sizes. "A" engines were the least powerful and "D" engines were badass. Some rockets also came with clear-plastic payloads, and more than once I sent a lizard into space. My reptilian astronauts never survived their flights and must have suffered horrifying deaths. I feel bad about it now, but as a boy it was just another day in paradise.

Being James Melvin, I couldn't bring myself to stop at just an ordinary rocket. I had to build the biggest one possible, a four-foot-tall monstrosity powered by four D engines. It was the Estes rocket equivalent of NASA's Saturn V—so big, in fact, that I didn't dare launch it on the island. There was no telling how high it would fly or where it might land. I needed an extremely large open area to test this behemoth.

My friend's dad drove us to a school with an open field with only a few scattered trees that spanned at least twenty acres. It was a Saturday, so the three of us were the only people there except for an old man who had a pitching wedge and a golf ball and was practicing his short game.

I set up the rocket and prepared it for launch. My friend and I were eager to see how high it would go, and even his dad seemed excited. But the guy with the pitching wedge wasn't paying us any attention. He was a thousand feet away from my launch pad, obliviously hitting a shot, walking to his ball, and hitting another. Practice makes perfect.

Meanwhile, the anticipation built at launch control. We counted down ten, nine, eight … but just before we shouted ONE, the cumbrous weight of the rocket caused the launch pad to topple over right as I pressed the ignition button.

Rather than soar into the sky, the rocket shot sideways and flew parallel to the ground like a guided missile. And when I say guided missile, I mean it. Those four D engines were not messing around. My Estes version of the Titanic blazed along at what seemed like 200 miles per hour.

Even worse, it flew straight at the golfer.

"LOOK OUUUUTTTT!!!!" I screamed at the top of my lungs. But he didn't seem to hear. Luckily, the rocket remained about ten feet above the ground, roaring a few feet over his head before finally crashing into a lone tree and exploding into a million pieces.

Amazingly, the man only glanced at us for a few seconds and then went right back to practicing with his pitching wedge as if nothing unusual had happened.

I might be in prison right now if the rocket had killed him. Whew! Another disaster narrowly avoided.

Kites were another passion of mine. My favorite was a clear plastic kite with a realistic illustration—maybe a bit too realistic—of a bald eagle on it. One day I was in a field flying my eagle kite when a feisty mockingbird swooped in and attacked the eagle over and over. By the time I wound the kite back in, the mockingbird had torn the eagle half to shreds.

Up next is another example of me pushing the

envelope. One 500-foot spool of kite string didn't satisfy me. I had to have four. Our backyard faced east over Tampa Bay, and I waited until a day came when the wind was blowing hard from the west. Then I launched the kite into the sky and ended up using all 2,000 feet of string. I stood there and admired the kite for about thirty minutes before beginning the laborious process of reeling it in. But soon after I started, the string broke.

Rather than drop into the bay, the kite continued to soar, rising into the stratosphere until I could no longer see it at all.

Who knows where it ended up? Maybe it landed on the deck of a tanker headed to Port Tampa Bay. Or perhaps it sailed clear across the bay and fell next to a kid in his yard. Maybe that kid is now an older man like me and is writing his own memoir about the time he was playing alone in his backyard and a kite floated down and landed magically at his feet.

Or maybe the kite is still in the sky and headed to distant stars.

INTERLUDE VI

Mom gets fired up and decides to paint my bedroom. Everything is white, including new white curtains. My room hasn't looked this good ... ever. My friend comes over to check out my new digs. After a few oohs and ahhs, we go back to doing what boys our age always do: figuring out a way to entertain ourselves. Somewhere along the way, we get into an epic sword fight with a pair of magic markers, caps off. It goes on for about five minutes before we suddenly stop and gasp. Large portions of the walls, including those brand-new curtains, are sprinkled with black ink. This makes the Frisbee-on-the-roof incident look like small potatoes. Guess who repainted his room and paid for another set of curtains out of his own lawn-mowing money? Boys can be brave, inventive, and imaginative, but they can also be dumb as hell. It takes my mom quite a while to forgive me for that one.

THE GIANT SWEETART

There was a popular family restaurant in south St. Petersburg called Munch's. It was founded in the early Fifties and finally closed a couple of years ago. The locals loved it, and so did out-of-towners. I went there often when I was growing up. It was less than a two-mile bike ride from my house. For a quarter, I could get a frosty mug of the most delicious root beer on the planet. For two quarters, I could get two frosty mugs, and so on.

If I was flush that day, I'd ask them to add a scoop of vanilla ice cream. Yow!

The restaurant's namesake owner, Mr. Munch, has since passed away, but back in the late 1960s and early '70s he was almost always there, manning his old-fashioned cash register.

Munch's had a modest gift store where they sold souvenirs, postcards, and a variety of sweets. There was a basket next to the cash register filled with Giant SweeTARTs, which were the size of a hockey puck and took at least ten minutes to eat. It was time well spent.

One fateful afternoon, two of my friends and I came up with a crazy plan. We decided that each of us was going to steal a Giant SweeTART from the basket. Who knows why? I guess the thrill and challenge of a five-finger discount intrigued us.

After enjoying a mug of root beer, the three of us went to the gift store and pretended to look around. Our goal was to find an opening when no one was looking, snag one of the SweeTARTs, and casually walk out. The restaurant was busy, per usual, and a group of people were milling around the gift shop while others waited in line at the cash register. Our own milling stretched on for a suspiciously long time.

One of my friends saw an opening, grabbed a SweeTART, and slipped out the door. A while after that, my second friend did the same, leaving me with two choices: Complete the heist or split with my tail between my legs. Being prideful and competitive, the latter was not an option. In a frantic moment, I grabbed a SweeTART and literally ran out the door.

My bike was nearby, and I jumped on it to make my escape. As I rode away, I glanced back at the glass door of the restaurant and saw Mr. Munch staring at me. He didn't look angry, just puzzled. It was like he was thinking, "Why would a nice boy like that steal something from me after all the frosty mugs of root beer we've served him?"

My friends were waiting for me around the corner, but I blew past them like I was on the penultimate leg of the Tour de France. I made it home in record time and hid in my bedroom, expecting the cops to show up at any moment and haul me away in handcuffs.

I don't think I even ate that Giant SweeTART. And if I did, I'm sure I didn't enjoy it. Even worse, I was terrified to go back to Munch's after my notorious deed. I lived the next two years of my life without root beers, hamburgers, bacon and eggs, and all the other delicious offerings served at Munch's. All that lost, for something that would have cost me 10 cents.

When I finally went back, my heart pounded out of my chest. But no one there, including Mr. Munch, paid me any attention. After that, it was like old times, restoring joy to the world. As you might imagine, I stole nothing from Munch's again, but I became one of the restaurant's best tippers, paying back their 10-cent loss a thousand times over.

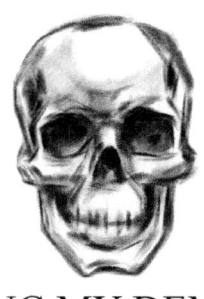

FACING MY DEMONS

Nowadays, young kids are overly exposed to violent entertainment, whether in movies, on TV, or via a plethora of online venues. I find this disheartening. How can it not have negative effects on our children and grandchildren?

However, in the Sixties it wasn't like kids spent all their time dancing joyously in fields of sweet-smelling flowers, humming innocent lullabies, and hugging everyone in sight. Not even close. There was plenty of scary stuff being wired into our brains. One example is the original *Night of the Living Dead*, which I first watched at a drive-in movie theater when I was 12. I remember seeing it with my friend and one of his sisters who was just old enough to drive. After the movie, they dropped me off at the curb in front of my house and I raced through the zombie-infested darkness to my front door as fast as a bolt of lightning. I laugh when I watch that movie now, but I sure wasn't laughing then.

Other scary movies included *Rosemary's Baby*, *Psycho*, *The Boston Strangler*, and a bloodcurdling cluster of vampire, werewolf, and zombie flicks, not to mention TV shows such as *The Twilight Zone*, *Dark Shadows*, and *The Outer Limits*. You could make the argument that the 1960s was one of the creepiest decades ever.

For a boy like me with an imagination the size of a thundercloud, all this high-level spookiness made going to bed at night quite the emotional tribulation. There were monsters everywhere! And I was clearly their most sought-after victim.

But of course, James Melvin was not without a plan. During the safer daylight hours, I meticulously devised a system of defense against supernatural assaults that made crucifixes, wooden stakes, and strings of garlic look like child's play.

My mightiest talisman was a rubber frog with an

elastic band attached to the top of its head. The frog was thick and muscular with bulging eyes that shot laser beams at ill-intentioned entities. A powerhouse of that magnitude would cow even the most dangerous demon, so I put the frog in charge of my first line of defense, hanging him on the doorknob where he protected the entryway to my room with the resolve of a steely sentinel.

Protecting the door was a crucial first step, but my room had three other points of weakness that monsters might exploit. They could emerge from my closet, slip through my bedroom window, or crawl out from under my bed. These vulnerable areas needed heavy fortification before I could sleep without concern.

Do you remember my G.I. Joes from a previous chapter? As you know, they were warriors of high esteem—proud, fearless, and not to be taken lightly. I stationed three of them on my windowsill and six more in various positions beneath my bed. This alone provided significant protection, but I wasn't finished yet. Joining the G.I. Joes on the windowsill was a mishmash of magical trinkets: colorful seashells I had collected at St. Pete Beach; an opal ring I discovered half-buried in the dirt on the playground at school; a silver dollar I gleefully spotted glistening in the Kresge's parking lot; and a rusty pocketknife I found jammed in the back of the junk drawer in our kitchen.

And there was more! When I was young, I believed pennies were indeed lucky, and I picked them up whenever and wherever I saw them. These were used to line both the windowsill and the spaces between the G.I. Joes assigned to under-the-bed duty. I now felt that the door, window, and bed were secured. Only the closet remained.

Two movie posters taped to the closet door did the trick. One advertised *Mary Poppins,* who didn't take crap from anybody, much less a demon. The other poster was a brand-new one for the Steve McQueen movie *Bullitt*. Together, tough-girl Mary and tough-guy Steve were impregnable.

The only thing left was to place a few more lucky pennies underneath my closet door. Now my talismanic fortress was complete. The demons might kill my parents and sister, who weren't savvy enough to set up their own magical barriers, but the three of them didn't seem overly concerned about that, so I left them to their own devices.

My parents thought I was nuts. My sister agreed. But I didn't care. My life was at stake—my very soul, if you think about it—and I didn't take this lightly. Every night before bed, I checked to make sure the talismans were all in their proper positions. And lastly, I conferred with my general, the muscle-bound frog hanging on the doorknob. We stared at each other, eye to eye, brothers in a war against evil. Neither of us even blinked. Well, he didn't blink. I guess I might have.

The demons outside my door and window, in my closet, and under my bed moaned in dismay over their inability to devour me. But their wanton cries carried little threat. My magic was the greater.

I rested my head on the pillow and slept well.

LIFE-SAVER

When I was 10, I was a big fan of the 1960s pop rock band The Monkees. I fell in love with the group's first album cleverly titled *The Monkees* and played it over and over on my portable record player, which I carried around like a small suitcase. I also loved the band's TV show. Back then, even the cool kids liked The Monkees.

The 1967 release of the band's second album *More of the Monkees* (another clever title!) was a big-time event for a superfan like me. Months ahead of the album's debut, I started saving every penny of my weekly 25-cent allowance. Eventually I had scrounged over two dollars in coins that I kept in a plastic sandwich bag. (This was so long ago, plastic sandwich bags were a relatively new invention.) I then called my local Kresge's dime store and asked how much the album cost. I was told $1.99 plus tax for a grand total of $2.03. I carefully counted my coins.

$2.40.

I had enough! With plenty leftover to buy a celebratory Coke and a bag of Lay's potato chips. I had a good life!

On a Saturday morning around 9, I asked my mom if I could ride my bike to Kresge's to buy the album. It was a mile and a half trek on roads that rarely had much traffic on weekends, so my mom thought nothing of it. As I've described in previous chapters, things were different back then. I rode my bike all over the place when I was as young as 8. Because physical exercise was built into our daily existences, most kids my age were in superb physical shape. We ran, swam, played crazy games, and spent most of our time outdoors. We were like miniature Olympians.

It was a sunny day in early February 1967. In many areas of the country, it would have been snowing, but on this day in Florida it was about 65 degrees, which felt cool and crisp to me.

I leaped on my bike and took off at full speed, streaking across Coquina Key like a man on a mission. I had about a mile to go to reach one of the short bridges that crossed over to the mainland, then another half mile to Kresge's. It would take me ten minutes to get there.

I was excited!

Then the unthinkable happened. Halfway there, I realized I had forgotten to bring my money. I had been in such a rush, I left the house without it.

Stupid!

Without even glancing to see if a car was coming, I made a looping U-turn across the street.

There was a terrible screeching of brakes.

I turned to see a black sedan heading straight for me, driven by a middle-aged woman. To this day, I can picture the horrified expression on her face, which was so contorted it barely looked human.

The rear of her car slid to the left, causing the front of the car to shift to the right, which might have been what saved me. The front bumper missed me by less than a foot. I then had to swerve my bike to miss the rear bumper, again by less than a foot. The car slammed to a halt. I skidded to a stop about twenty feet down the road.

I expected her to get out of her car and yell at me for being so reckless. Instead, she rolled down her window, twisted her head around, and asked me in a tender voice if I was okay.

"Yes ma'am," I said. And added, "Sorry."

She nodded, then drove slowly away.

Being a kid who grew up in the 1960s, the car incident barely fazed me. Heck, I had spent my childhood swimming in shark-infested waters, climbing 100-foot trees, huddling in underground forts that could have collapsed on me at any moment, and frequently being chased by snarling dogs. In comparison, the car thing didn't seem worse than any other.

I pedaled home, got my money, and made it back to Kresge's before 10 a.m. Then I zoomed home with my album, a Coke, and a bag of chips and spent the rest of the day listening to such classic hits as *She*;

Mary, Mary; *I'm Not Your Stepping Stone*; and *I'm a Believer*.

I remember *She* had these lyrics:

Sheeeeeeeeeee told me that she loved me. And like a fool I believed her from the start.

As boys, we of course twisted the lyrics to:

Sheeeeeeeeee told me that she loved me. And then she turned around and cut a fart.

It inspired hysterical laughter every time.

But I digress.

Though it made little impression on me when it first happened, the near-death incident grew on my mind. If things had gone differently, few of the adventures I've described in my *Florida Boy* memoir would have occurred. What happened on that sunny day when I was a little kid is the closest I've come to dying.

The woman who nearly hit me would now be almost 100, so she is most likely no longer among us. But I often think about her. Did she ever wonder about the little boy whose life she saved? I'd like to think she did. I owe her one.

EPILOGUE

Some might ask why I still identify as a Florida boy when I haven't lived in the state for over two decades. In fact, I wasn't even born there. My hometown is Poughkeepsie, New York, but my family moved to Florida when I was 5 and I remained in the Sunshine State for forty-plus years. I lived on Coquina Key in St. Petersburg from 1962-1978 and stayed in or near St. Pete until 2004. For personal reasons, I moved to Upstate SC after that and have called this area my home ever since. Though I'm now happily retired in the mountains, Florida is still dear to my heart.

As I write this now, Year 2024 is coming to an end. Hurricane Helene has recently thundered through the Eastatoee Valley and left the forests in ruins. My house in the valley escaped mostly unscathed, but my fifteen acres of tree-laden land look like Vladimir Putin dropped an atomic bomb on them. My wife and I own a full-house generator—so we weren't exactly suffering—but we otherwise had no external power, internet, or cell signal for over two weeks.

Ironically, during my forty-plus years in the Tampa Bay area, there was never a direct hit from a hurricane. Not until I moved 400 miles inland from the Gulf of Mexico did a hurricane manage to nail me head on. In further irony, the Tampa Bay area—including Coquina Key—was also blasted by Helene (and later Milton). Many homes on Coquina Key were damaged by a horrific one-two punch. I wish for quick recoveries for where I now live and for my former home. Life goes on even in the worst of times.

As for my own life, I've raised a family while working for decades at several highly demanding jobs. I've also managed to write ten published novels and three novellas. Some of my older works are going to be re-released in 2025, which thrills me to no end.

The Adventures of a Florida Boy is my first memoir. Compared to most of my other books, it's a short little thing. Yet it has more than its share of nostalgic charm.

This memoir was first published in serial form in my free Substack newsletter called *Jim Melvin's Realms of Fantasy.* The serialization received a decent amount of attention and attracted a loyal following. If you're reading this, you know who you are.

Like any person, I've accomplished less than some and more than others. I have my good points and bad. Some love me, some not so much, and most couldn't give a crap. For those who love me, I love you back. For those I've harmed, I beg your forgiveness. For those who don't give a crap, that's okay. It's impossible to keep track of everyone.

I grew up during a time when imagination is what got me through the day. It flourished in fantastical fashion and has remained with me into old age.

As I mentioned at the beginning of this book, today's world has an overabundance of hatred and hopelessness. It seems that our own nation has never been less united. The future has a bleak look to it.

Which brings me back to why I love this book. My stories are from a bygone era we will never see again, a time when life was simpler and more innocent. For me, reliving these memories has been a refreshing break from today's drama and trauma. I hope it has had a similar effect on you by awakening the fondest memories of your own childhood.

Life is what it is.

For better or worse.

And it all begins when we're young.

Get to know Jim Melvin

Jim is a novelist who now lives in the foothills of the Southern Appalachians, though he spent more than forty years of his life in St. Petersburg, Florida. He is the author of *The Death Wizard Chronicles*, a six-book epic fantasy for mature audiences. New editions of this series will debut in 2025.

Once upon a time, Jim's youngest daughter asked him to write a series more appropriate for her age group. Hence, *Dark Circles* was born. The teen fantasy adventure series is for readers 13 and older.

Similarly, Jim's wife was the driving force behind *The Adventures of a Florida Boy*. She enjoyed hearing stories about his childhood and encouraged him to write about them.

Jim has been a professional writer for most of his life. He was an award-winning journalist at several large newspapers and a communications director at a major university. He has written more than a thousand articles for newspapers and magazines.

Please leave a review

If you've gotten this far, I'm assuming you've read *The Adventures of a Florida Boy*.

Please take a minute to post an online review or rating.

Thank you!

–Jim Melvin

Subscribe to Jim's newsletter
Realms of Fantasy at jim-melvin.com.
Be sure to click on the NEWSLETTER tab
at the top of the home page.
All of the newsletter's content is free.

Novels by Jim Melvin

Dark Circles (13 and older)

Winner of 14 international awards
Available now:
Book 1: *Do You Believe in Magic?*
Book 2: *Do You Believe in Monsters?*
Book 3: *Do You Believe in Miracles?*

The Death Wizard Chronicles (18 and older)

New editions coming soon:
Book 1: *Forged in Death*
Book 2: *Chained by Fear*
Book 3: *Shadowed by Demons*
Book 4: *Torn by War*
Book 5: *Blinded by Power*
Book 6: *Healed by Hope*

Nonfiction books

- *Eclipse Over Clemson*
- *The Adventures of a Florida Boy*

Acknowledgements

The Adventures of a Florida Boy had seven Beta readers. What a privilege … thank you! Each reader contributed something to this book. In their honor, here they are:

Sharon Burke, Linda Chrisman, Jenn Herl, Sarah Hylton, Garrett Lawlor, Janet Morris, Marybeth Rubinacci.

Special thanks to my wife Jeanne Malmgren for her encouragement, editing, and overall expertise.

Thanks also to the unnamed childhood friends who played starring roles in this memoir.

Finally, a nod to the universe for not inventing video games, home computers, and smartphones until after I had mostly finished growing up.

Printed in Great Britain
by Amazon